He Healed Them All

He Healed Them All

How to lay hold of your healing

Anthony Reinglas

Xtreme Publishing House

Many who know me are aware that most all of my current writings, teachings and preaching is most specifically about the Kingdom of God, what it is, how it operates and how to live your life in a way that is reflective of this Kingdom. My daily prayer and desire is to know Him (My God, My Lord (King) and Savior, and for daily knowledge and wisdom concerning His Kingdom and His righteousness. After all, He tells us specifically in Mathew 6:33 to seek this first in life, and then everything else will be added to us, so why seek anything else?

To live a life reflective or representative of the Kingdom of God we must know the attributes of the Kingdom. Prosperity (of every kind), mental and emotional wholeness, divine health, and chiefly having and living in total dominion and authority over this natural decaying realm and earthly Kingdom. Notice I did not just say healing, I said divine health? That's because healing is not an attribute of the Kingdom, divine health is. Something or someone needing healing would indicate that there is something presently imperfect within the Kingdom. So healing is something that should come as we enter the Kingdom; and into Gods perfect will which is for you to walk and live in divine health from then forward, so you then can lay hands on the sick and bring them into the Kingdom of God, just as Jesus did.

God spoke to me one morning (this morning actually) and gave me everything that I am writing in this book. He illuminated this to me early this morning and then told me to write this book today, design the covers, edit and publish it within 24 hours. Today is Thursday, the Thursday before Easter (Resurrection) Sunday. Technically this is the day Jesus ate His Passover meal with the disciples and was arrested in the garden of

Gethsemane... tomorrow is Good Friday and Sunday is coming! So I feel especially empowered as I am writing this because Gods timing is so amazing to me in that during the same relative time Jesus is being beaten, whipped and scourged for your healing, He gave me this to write and give to you!

There are many people pleading with God for healing in the body of Christ and asking God for a divine miracle healing in their life so they can be rid of what ever ailment it may be that plagues them. If this is you today, I want to start off (and assert) that for those who are not Christians, healing is a miracle. In fact, many times healing is the very miracle Jesus used to bring people to know His Love. Also understand that believing in Jesus is not a prerequisite for healing; Jesus healed many who were not believers.. some who had no idea even who he was! But it is the goodness of God that leads men to repentance (Romans 2:4)... This is also the reason when taking communion and celebrating Christ, we take the Body first, then the Blood..

So when Paul states in:

1 Corinthians 11:29-30 "...For he who eats and drinks in an unworthy manner eats and drinks judgment to himself, not discerning the Lord's body. For this reason many *are* weak and sick among you, and many sleep."

Many religious people preach and teach this from an erroneous or ignorant view and I just want to tell you what *it does* mean... Notice that he does not mention the blood here, only the body, why? Because he states that many are weak and sick and many die because they do not understand that the Body of Christ was broken whipped, beaten and scourged for your healing, and because He did that for you, there is no need for you to ever be sick a day in your life! This is your absolute right when you become a Christian and citizen of the Kingdom of God.

So when you are a Christian, healing is not a miracle as it is for non-Christians, it's a right of passage and your responsibility even to walk in it, just as it is your responsibility to walk in forgiveness and love. Read that again if you need to, because it is important to understand the right to healing and wholeness you have as a believer.

We are in a time in America where the present Administration is intentionally opening the borders of this Country and allowing illegal immigration to flood this Nation. The immigrants are bringing in crime, disease, corruption and a general lack of order and morals. This is the mass of them and certainly not all.. I bring this up because it has been upsetting me to the point of losing some sleep on occasion. It upset me to see people who do nothing for this Country come in and get benefits, money, healthcare and even housing and act as if we owe them this. Well, last night was one of those nights I lost some sleep.

Now you can think that this is not a great attitude to have, but please understand that even the Kingdom of God/Heaven has borders... The only difference between a lake and a swamp is that one has borders and one does not.

So getting back on track! God woke me this morning and said plainly.. This is that mindset

Christians should have upon entering the Kingdom. I said WHAT? He showed me in my mind my medical card...

> And said *When you go to the doctor you expect treatment, you expect to be seen, diagnosed, treated and given a prescription if needed don't you?*

I said "Yes Lord I do, that's what I pay for"
> *So you expect it, and if they do not provide the service you will go so far as to get adamant and demand that they see you and provide that service, and then even fight if need be for it to be covered, don't you?*

Yes, of course
> *So when these immigrants come into the country, they know the rights given to them but you get mad at them for receiving what the government gives them freely. Can you blame them? This is in part the meaning of Luke 16:8"* For the

sons of this world are more shrewd in their generation than the sons of light."

OK Lord, what's your point?

> *When you come into the Kingdom of God, you have certain rights. You are given a new health card written in My Word (Isaiah 53:4-5) and yet most do not discern it or take advantage of it. Its your right, fight for it like you do anything else.*

Then He left me hanging and my mind has been going since!

Let's take a look at Isaiah 53:4-5...

Surely He has borne our [1]griefs
And carried our sorrows;
Yet we esteemed Him stricken,
Smitten by God, and afflicted.
[5] But He *was* wounded for our transgressions,
He was bruised for our iniquities;
The chastisement for our peace *was* upon Him,
And by His stripes we are healed.

Allow me to read this in the NLT for better understanding:

Yet it was our weaknesses he carried;
it was our sorrows that weighed him down.
And we thought his troubles were a punishment from God,
a punishment for his own sins!
⁵ But he was pierced for our rebellion,
crushed for our sins.
He was beaten so we could be whole.
He was whipped so we could be healed.

And the Amplified says: The punishment [required] for our well-being *fell* on Him..
Do you get that?

So I want you to understand and know that just as a Father cares for his child and wants them well all the time, so does your heavenly Father. Please know also that He does not put sickness upon anyone for any reason at all, and especially not to teach them something! This is a demonic teaching that has infiltrated some churches and lie from hell. If any parent left their kid outside so they catch cold for the purposes of teaching them something, Social Services should come and take that child away because that's abuse! God is a loving and caring God and a good, good Father!

There is no sickness in heaven, and since the Kingdom of God on this earth is to be a mirror and in agreement with the Kingdom of Heaven, there is no sickness that should overtake you here either. So as you enter into the citizenship of the Kingdom of God, by virtue of becoming Born Again, it becomes your right as a citizen to not only be healed, but to walk in divine health. That's what Christ did for you; and for you not to take it is to let Him do it all in vain.

Now I understand that most people have gone through a lifetime of negative programing from society, the worldly healthcare system and even churches sometimes.. so I placed some scriptures below for you to read, recite, dwell on and get into your spirit. Read then and confess then daily if you need to, and please email us your testimonies through our website.

Before I list them, Let's pray together in agreement that Gods Word will be planted on good ground (your heart) and take root.. His Word will never return void and will always accomplish what it set out to do... so lets pray:

If you have not yet made Him your Lord and Savior:

Heavenly Father I come before you and confess that I am a sinner and ask you to forgive me now for my sins, I ask that you come into my heart: I believe in Jesus Christ as your Son make Hiim my Lord and Savior today and all the days of my life. I ask that You fill me with your Holy Spirit to lead me and guide me today and all the days of my life and ask that you help me to hear His voice in this busy world and to be an effective witness for you and your Kingdom.

All:

Lord God I come boldly before your throne of Grace and ask in the Righteousness imparted though your Son Jesus Christ that you hear my prayer. I pray for not only healing today but for wholeness, and for your living Word and Love to envelope me from the top of my head to the tip of my toes and for every cell in my body to line up with, and come in agreement with the truth of your Word and Kingdom.

I ask that you help me to be a conduit of your love and healing to others as well as to expand your Kingdom and the knowledge of your Son Jesus Christ.

Praise God!

Now lets read and confess these scriptures as often as needed to get them into your spirit!

"'If you can'?" said Jesus. "***Everything* is possible for one who believes.**" Mark 9:23

Isaiah 53:4-5

Surely He has borne our griefs And carried our sorrows; Yet we esteemed Him stricken, Smitten by God, and afflicted. But He *was* wounded for our transgressions, *He was* bruised for our iniquities; The chastisement for our peace *was* upon Him, And by His stripes we are healed.

Isaiah 41:10

Fear not, for I am with you; be not dismayed, for I am your God. I will strengthen you, yes, I will help you, I will uphold you with my righteous right hand.

Psalm 30:2

LORD my God, I called to you for help, and you healed me.

Matthew 11:28

Come to me, all you who are weary and burdened, and I will give you rest

Isaiah 57:18-19

I have seen their ways, but I will heal them; I will

guide them and restore comfort to Israel's mourners, creating praise on their lips. Peace, peace, to those far and near," says the LORD. "And I will heal them."

Jeremiah 17:14

Heal me, O Lord, and I will be healed; save me and I will be saved, for you are the one I praise."

Jeremiah 30:17

But I will restore you to health and heal your wounds,' declares the LORD.

Jeremiah 33:6

Behold, I will bring to it health and healing, and I will heal them and reveal to them abundance of prosperity and security.

Exodus 23:25

Worship the LORD your God, and his blessing will be on your food and water. I will take away sickness from among you

Isaiah 41:10

So do not fear, for I am with you; do not be dismayed, for I am your God. I will strengthen you and help you; I will uphold you with my righteous right hand.

Psalm 41:3:

The Lord sustains him on his sickbed; in his illness you restore him to full health.

Psalm 103:2-3

Bless the Lord, O my soul, and forget not all his benefits, who forgives all your iniquity, who heals all your diseases,

Psalm 147:3

He heals the brokenhearted and binds up their wounds.

3 John 1:2

Beloved, I pray that all may go well with you and that you may be in good health, as it goes well with your soul.

Philippians 4:19

And my God will meet all your needs according to the riches of his glory in Christ Jesus.

1Peter 2:24

He himself bore our sins in his body on the tree, that we might die to sin and live to righteousness. By His wounds you have been healed.

James 5:14-15

Is anyone among you sick? Let them call the elders of the church to pray over them and anoint them with oil in the name of the Lord. And the prayer offered in faith will make the sick person well; the Lord will raise them up. If they have sinned, they will be forgiven.

Proverbs 17:22

A cheerful heart is good medicine, but a crushed spirit dries up the bones.

Psalm 34:17-18

The righteous cry out, and the LORD hears them; he delivers them from all their troubles. The

LORD is close to the brokenhearted and saves those who are crushed in spirit.

Isaiah 40:29,31

He gives power to the weak, and to those who have no might He increases strength...Those who wait on the LORD shall renew their strength; they shall mount up with wings like eagles, they shall run and not be weary, they shall walk and not faint.

Psalm 119:50

This is my comfort in my affliction, that your promise gives me life." —

Psalm 147:3

He heals the brokenhearted and binds up their wounds.

Psalm 103:2-4

Praise the LORD, my soul, and forget not all his benefits —who forgives all your sins and heals all your diseases, who redeems your life from the pit and crowns you with love and compassion.

3 John 1:2

Beloved, I pray that all may go well with you and that you may be in good health, as it goes well with your soul.

Malachi 4:2

But for you who fear My name, the sun of righteousness shall rise with healing in its wings. You shall go out leaping like calves from the stall.

Matthew 9:35

<u>Jesus went through all the towns and villages, teaching in their synagogues, proclaiming the good news of the kingdom and healing every disease and sickness.</u>

Luke 6:19

And the people all tried to touch him, because power was coming from him **and healing them all.**

Proverbs 3:5-8

Trust in the LORD with all your heart, and lean not on your own understanding. In all your ways submit to him, and he will make your paths straight. Do not be wise in your own eyes; fear the LORD and shun evil. This will bring health to your body and nourishment to your bones.

Exodus 23:25

Worship the LORD your God, and his blessing will be on your food and water. I will take away sickness from among you..

Proverbs 4:20-22

My son, give attention to my words; incline your ear to my sayings. Do not let them depart from your eyes; keep them in the midst of your heart; for they are life to those who find them, and health to all their flesh.

Isaiah 58:8

Then your light will break forth like the dawn, and your healing will quickly appear; then your righteousness will go before you, and the glory of the Lord will be your rear guard.

If this book has blessed you, I encourage you to leave an honest review on Amazon or Google to help us and help others find it.

If you have not yet ordered a copy of my new book, *The Kingdom, the Power & the Glory: Manifesting the Kingdom of God*, get it now! This highly informative new book, will explain the Kingdom of God like never before and unlock some secrets, doors and keys to the Kingdom that will fuel and ignite your walk, mission and purpose while allowing you to live in a way that will blow people's minds!

All things for the Kingdom
Anthony Reinglas

Anthony
Reinglas
Amazon
Author Page

Link to my
Amazon
author page

Xtreme1038.com

AnthonyReinglas.com

I Missed the Rapture -
Imissedtherapture.com

Gods 4 Me - Gods4Me.com